The Heinemann Illustrated Encyclopedia

Volume 4
Eye-Hip

First published in Great Britain by Heinemann Library
Halley Court, Jordan Hill, Oxford OX2 8EJ
a division of Reed Educational and Professional Publishing Ltd.

OXFORD MELBOURNE AUCKLAND
JOHANNESBURG BLANTYRE GABORONE
IBADAN PORTSMOUTH NH (USA) CHICAGO

Series Editors: Rebecca and Stephen Vickers
Author Team: Rob Alcraft, Catherine Chambers, Jim Drake,
Fred Martin, Angela Royston, Jane Shuter, Roger Thomas,
Rebecca Vickers, Stephen Vickers
Reading Consultant: Betty Root

Photo research by Katharine Smith
Illustration on page 20 by Ray Webb, Oxford Illustrators
Designed and Typeset by Gecko Ltd
Printed in Hong Kong by Wing King Tong

02 01 00 99 98
10 9 8 7 6 5 4 3 2 1

ISBN 0 431 09055 6

British Library Cataloguing in Publication Data.

The Heinemann illustrated encyclopedia
   1. Children's encyclopedias and dictionaries
   I. Vickers, Rebecca II. Vickers, Stephen, 1951–
032

ISBN 0431090629

Acknowledgements:
Cover: The cover illustration is of a male specimen of *Ornithoptera goliath*, commonly called
the Goliath Birdwing. Special thanks to Dr George C. McGavin and the Hope Entomological Collections,
Oxford University Museum of Natural History.

J. Allan Cash Ltd: pp7t, 9, 17, 26, 28, 29, 34, 35, 36, 47. **Ancient Art and Architecture:** Mary Jelcliffe – p46.
Ardea London Ltd: J. M. Labat – p12b; Valerie Taylor – p12t. **Bridgeman Art Library:** p5. **BBC Natural
History Unit:** John Cancalosi – p22t; Jeff Rotman – p11b. **Trevor Clifford Photography:** pp24, 24b. **Bruce
Coleman:** Wayne Larkinen – p45t. **FLPA:** Fritz Polking – p10b. **Ronald Grant Archive:** Walt Disney Co – p6b.
Hulton Deutsch: p44t. **The Hutchinson Library:** Sarah Errington – p38. **Oxford Scientific Films:** Jen and
Den Bartlett – p32; G. I. Bernard – p25b; Mike Birkhead – p45b; Roger Brown – p27b; George Bruce – p18;
Alan and Sandy Carey – p23b; Bruce Davidson – p48t; Tim Davis – p30t; Mark Deebie and Victoria Stone –
p14t; Jack Dermid – p25t; Paul Franklin – p21t; Jim Frazer – p40b; David Fritts – p31b; Christian Gazimek –
p20; Mike Hill – p14b; Tim Jackson – p30b; Paul Kay – p37b; Michael Leach – p4; Renee Lynn – p23t;
Alistair McEwan – p15; Sean Morris – p33b; Owen Newman – p43; Richard Parkwood – p48b; Hans
Reinhard – p21b; James Robinson – p31t; Survival Anglia – 39b (T. Andrewartha), 39t (Claude Steelman);
Charles Tyler – p7b; Peter Ward – p27t; Martin Wendler – p33t; M. Wilding – p40t. **Redferns:** p19. **Science
Photo Library:** Agema Infrared Systems – p42t; Deep Light Industries – p41; Simon Fraser – p8. **Tony Stone
Worldwide:** Ary Diesendruck – p16t; Alan Hicks – p44b; Alan Thornton – p13. **Sygma:** p16.

Every effort has been made to contact copyright holders of any material
reproduced in this book. Any omissions will be rectified in subsequent
printings if notice is given to the Publisher.

Welcome to the
Heinemann Illustrated Encyclopedia

What is an encyclopedia?

An encyclopedia is an information book. It gives the most important facts about a lot of different subjects. This encyclopedia has been specially written for children your age. It covers many of the subjects from school and others you may find interesting.

What is in this encyclopedia?

In this encyclopedia each topic is called an entry. There is one page for every entry. The entries in this encyclopedia are on:

- animals
- plants
- dinosaurs
- countries
- geography
- history
- world religions
- music
- art
- transport
- science
- technology

How to use this encyclopedia

This encyclopedia has eleven books, called volumes. The first ten volumes contain entries. The entries are all in alphabetical order. This means that Volume One starts with entries that begin with the letter 'A' and Volume Ten ends with entries that begin with the letter 'Z'. Volume Eleven is the index volume and has some other interesting information in its Fact Finder section.

Here are two entries, showing you what you can find on a page:

The See also line tells you where to find other related information.

This is the letter that the entry starts with.

Fact boxes give you details about the topic.

Did You Know? boxes have fun or interesting bits of information.

The Fact File tells you important facts and figures.

Eye

See also: Animal, Human body

Eyes are used by animals to see. Eyes catch the light that bounces off an object and make an image of it. Most parts of the human eye are hidden inside the head to keep them safe.

Eye problems

If the lens of the eye is the wrong shape, it can't make a clear image. The eye cannot focus. Glasses and contact lenses can help the eyes to focus properly.

DID YOU KNOW?

Nocturnal animals that go out to hunt at night have special pupils in their eyes that open very wide. This lets in as much light as possible.

The owl has big pupils that help it to see very clearly in the dark.

Parts of the human eye

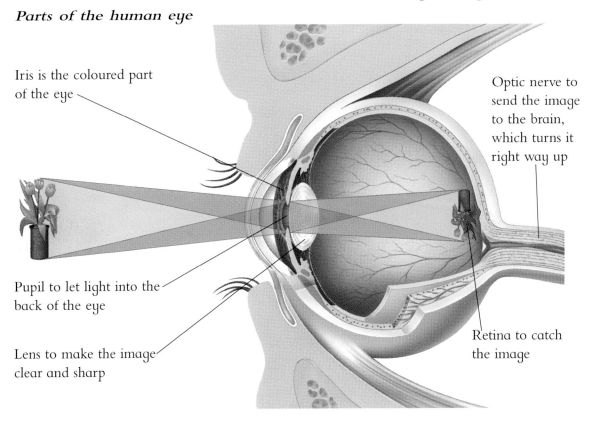

Iris is the coloured part of the eye

Optic nerve to send the image to the brain, which turns it right way up

Pupil to let light into the back of the eye

Lens to make the image clear and sharp

Retina to catch the image

Fable

See also: Literature, Story

A fable is a short story which tries to teach an important lesson about life. The characters in fables are often animals, but they behave and talk like people. The lesson the fable teaches is called the moral.

Who wrote fables?

The most famous fable writers are Aesop, Jean de la Fontaine and Lessing. La Fontaine lived in France in the 1800s, and Gotthold Ephraim Lessing, lived in Germany about a hundred years later. In India about 1500 years ago, a wise man called Bidpai wrote a collection of animal fables. Bidpai used these to explain how a young prince should lead his life.

The stories of all of these writers have been translated into many languages.

This is an illustration made over 200 years ago for the fable 'The Fox and the Grapes'.

DID YOU KNOW?

In one of Aesop's stories the fox finds an actor's mask, with holes for the eyes and mouth. 'Ah!' says the fox to the mask, 'You are beautiful on the outside, but behind your face there is nothing!' The moral is that people should not worry about how they look, but about the way they behave.

Aesop (620–560BC)

Aesop was a storyteller in Ancient Greece. He probably lived his life as a slave on the island of Samos. Aesop wrote a famous collection of animal fables.

Fairy tale

See also: Literature, Story

Fairy tales are stories for children. Not all fairy tales are about fairies. They are usually about magic or imaginary creatures. Some of the stories are set in the past, but fairy tales can also be set in the present. Fairy stories have been told for hundreds of years.

Hans Christian Andersen wrote many famous fairy tales including 'The Princess and the Pea' and 'The Ugly Duckling'.

Who wrote fairy tales?

Some of the most famous fairy tales were collected and published by the Grimm brothers in the 1800s. Hans Christian Andersen lived in Denmark in the 1800s. He wrote 150 fairy tales, including 'Thumbelina', a story about a tiny girl.

Jacob Grimm
(1785–1863)

Wilhelm Grimm
(1786–1859)

The Grimm brothers were both interested in old fairy tales and they collected some that had been known for hundreds of years. The Grimm brothers wrote the stories in a book called *Tales from the Brothers Grimm*. These stories include 'Hansel and Gretel' and 'Snow White'.

The Grimm Brothers' 'Snow White' was used by Walt Disney to make this famous film in 1937.

Farming

See also: Crop, Soil, Weather

Farming is the work that people do to provide food and other crops. In some places, farmers and their families eat most of what they grow. In others, farmers grow crops to sell.

Types of farming

Farmers can grow food such as grains, fruit and vegetables. They can grow crops that are used to make other products, such as, cotton, tobacco, or even flowers. Farmers can also raise animals.

These rice fields in Nepal are flooded before the plants are stuck in by hand.

Some farmers use expensive machinery like this combine harvester to help do the farm work.

People and farming

People have been farming for over 9000 years. Some farmers do most of the work by hand, using tools such as forks and spades. Other farmers use machinery, such as tractors and harvesters. Special chemicals called fertilizers are used to help crops grow. Chemicals called insecticides and pesticides can be used to kill weeds and insects. Some farmers do not use chemicals. They believe it is bad for the land and may be harmful to people. This is called organic farming.

DID YOU KNOW?

More people in the world work in farming than in any other job.

Fern

See also: Plant

A fern is a green plant that does not have any flowers. Ferns grow in most parts of the world except for deserts. They grow best in damp, shady places.

Life of a fern

A fern produces spores instead of seeds. The spores are blown in the wind. When a spore falls to the ground, it grows into a small leaf, shaped like a heart. This leaf contains the male and female seeds. When a male seed and a female seed join together they grow into a new fern.

Ferns were one of the first kinds of plant to grow on land. Millions of years ago, when the dinosaurs were alive, giant tree ferns covered much of the land. Today people grow ferns in their gardens and as house plants.

FERN FACTS

NUMBER OF KINDS.....about 10,000
HEIGHT.......2.5 cm–25 m
LIFE SPAN.... up to 100 years
ENEMIES...... Some animals eat ferns.

The largest ferns are tree ferns which grow in hot, tropical countries. Tree ferns are one of the oldest types of plant still alive.

Leaf called a frond has many smaller leaflets

Spores are found on the underside of each leaflet

A frond of a lady fern

Finland

See also: Arctic, Europe

Finland is a country in northern Europe. It is mostly low, flat land, with some hills and mountains in the north. There are many lakes and forests. Summers are warm and winters are very cold, with snow.

Living and working

Most people in Finland live in cities in the south of the country. In the countryside, people live in traditional houses made of wood. A traditional meal is potatoes served with meat or fish, such as herrings. The people of Finland have a stringed instrument, called a *kantele*. As it is played, someone reads ancient poems.

Farmers in Finland grow cereals and root crops, and reindeer are reared for their meat. Around the coast, fish are caught and processed. Many people work in factories that make paper, print books and magazines and make other things out of wood.

Laplanders use boats on the many lakes. These people are wearing traditional dress.

DID YOU KNOW?

Lapland is in the north of Finland. The people there herd reindeer and catch fish. Laplanders live in the north of Norway, Sweden and Russia as well.

EUROPE

FACT FILE

PEOPLE .... Finnish, Finns

POPULATION .... 5.1 million

MAIN LANGUAGES .... Finnish, Swedish

CAPITAL CITY .... Helsinki

MONEY .... Markka

HIGHEST MOUNTAIN ... Haltiatunturi – 1324 m

LONGEST RIVER .... River Tornio – 410 km

Firefly

See also: Beetle, Insect

A firefly is a kind of beetle which gives off a glowing or flashing light. Fireflies live all over the world, except in Antarctica.

Firefly families

A female firefly lays her eggs in a damp place on the soil. The eggs hatch into glow-worms. Each glow-worm feeds and grows for about two years before changing into a pupa and then into a firefly. An adult firefly lives only from a few days to a month.

FIREFLY FACTS

NUMBER OF KINDS	1900
COLOUR	brown or black with red, yellow or orange markings
LENGTH	0.5-2 cm
STATUS	common
LIFE SPAN	up to 2 years
ENEMIES	birds, lizards, frogs, spiders

The underbelly of a Jamaican firefly

Soft but tough skin to protect the body

Yellowy-green flashing light for attracting a mate

Hard wing case covers and protects the wings

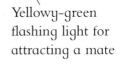

Fireflies fly around in the early evening. The adult males flash their lights to attract mates. Moving fireflies make the streaks of light in this photograph.

FOOD

A glow-worm eats flowers, snails, earthworms and caterpillars. It kills its food by injecting it with poison. Some adult fireflies do not eat at all, but others feed on nectar, a sweet juice made by some flowers.

Fish

See also: Fish (tropical), Sea life

A fish is an animal with fins, gills and a backbone. Fish live wherever there is water, almost everywhere around the world. Many fish live in the seas and oceans. Others live in ponds, lakes, rivers and streams.

Fish families

A female fish lays her eggs in the water. When the eggs hatch, the young fish feed on the egg yolk until they are old enough to find their own food. Most young fish are called fry. Some fish live on their own, but others swim in big groups called shoals.

FISH FACTS

NUMBER
OF KINDS.....over 20,000

COLOUR..... all colours and patterns

LENGTH...... 10mm–12m

WEIGHT......up to 15 tonnes

STATUS........common

LIFE SPAN.... up to 50 years

ENEMIES...... other fish, squid, people

Back and anal fins stop the fish rolling over

Gills take in oxygen from the water

Tail and tail fin move from side to side to push it through the water.

Hard scales for protection

Fins for steering

A cod fish

Fish like these glassy sweepers swim in large groups.

FOOD

Most fish hunt other fish and sea animals. Many have sharp teeth. Some fish also feed on water plants, and on tiny plants and animals called plankton.

Fish, tropical

See also: Coral, Fish, Sea life

Tropical fish are small, colourful fishes that live in warm waters in South America, Africa and southern Asia. Many people now keep tropical fish in aquariums, as pets.

Tank life

Only fish that like the same kind of water can live together in the same tank. Most tropical fish like warm water, but some kinds like cooler water. Some can only live in salt water. Some tropical fish, like piranhas, are so fierce that they have to be kept on their own.

Aquarium fish need to be fed with dried fish food. The tank must be kept clean and it must be big enough for the number of fish in it.

Tropical fish can be found in the wild, living where the water is warm. These fish live near a coral reef.

Plants and stones make the aquarium look nice and give the fish places to hide.

A small heater warms the water to keep it at the right temperature.

Air bubbles give the fish plenty of oxygen to breathe.

An aquarium for tropical fish.

Flag

See also: Communication

A flag is a piece of cloth with coloured patterns, shapes or symbols on it. Flags are flown using rope, poles or sticks, or they may hang down from buildings. People have used flags for more than a thousand years, as a way of saying something without using words.

The sailor uses two flags to send a message. The flags are held in different positions to show the letters of the alphabet. This is called semaphore.

FLAG FIRSTS

1777... The American flag was first used (the number of stars has changed over time)

1801... The modern British flag (the Union flag) was first used

1857... Flags were first used for international ship signalling

1863... The Red Cross flag was first used

1901... The modern Australian flag was first used

1914... The Olympic flag with five linking circles was first used

1948... The United Nations flag was first used

Using flags

Countries, parts of countries, international groups, clubs and teams can all have flags. It helps other people recognize what belongs to them, or who represents them.

In the past, armies carried flags when they fought. If a flag was captured by the enemy it usually meant that side won.

Ships from different countries can use special flags to signal to each other, even when the people don't speak the same language. A ship in trouble will hoist its flag upside down to let others know.

In motor racing the flags used to signal start, finish and danger are understood by all the people taking part.

Flamingo

See also: Bird

A flamingo is a tall, pink bird which lives in shallow, salty lakes. All flamingos live in warm countries.

Flamingo families

A flamingo lives in a huge flock, with thousands of other flamingos. Each pair of male and female flamingos builds a mud mound in shallow water. The female lays one egg in the nest. A baby flamingo is called a chick. Both parents take care of the chick until it has its proper feathers and can feed itself.

FOOD

Flamingos eat insect larvae, small crabs and shrimps. If a flamingo doesn't eat enough pink shrimps it loses its pink colour.

FLAMINGO FACTS

NUMBER OF KINDS	5
COLOUR	..... pink or pinkish-grey
HEIGHT	.... up to 150 cm
LENGTH	...... up to 165 cm
WEIGHT	......2–4 kg
STATUS	.... common
LIFE SPAN	.... about 10 years
ENEMIES	...... eagles, people

Beak for straining food from the water

Long neck for reaching down into the water for food

Long wings help this heavy bird to fly

long legs for wading through water and mud

A lesser flamingo

A female lesser flamingo with its chick.

Flea

See also: Insect

A flea is an insect that lives on the warm bodies of birds and mammals all over the world. Fleas are pests which suck the blood of the people and animals they live on. They can also carry diseases.

Flea families

Adult fleas lay their eggs in clothing, or in the nest or bedding of animals. A young flea first hatches into a larva. Three weeks to eight months later, the larva spins a cocoon. When it comes out of the cocoon it has changed into an adult. The adult must then quickly find a mammal or bird to live on.

FLEA FACTS

NUMBER OF KINDS	1800
COLOUR	black or brown
LENGTH	about 3 mm
STATUS	common
LIFE SPAN	nearly 2 years
ENEMIES	special chemicals called insecticides

hard body shell to protect it from animal scratching

A cat flea

FOOD

An adult flea sucks the blood of the animal it is living on. Flea larvae also feed on fallen hair, food scraps and other dirt.

Hard beak for piercing an animal's skin to suck its blood

Long, strong back legs for jumping more than 30 cm from one animal to another

Spikes on the legs for moving quickly through fur and feathers

This cat flea larva is feeding on blood.

Flood

See also: Coast, River, Weather

A flood is caused when water flows over the land. Floods can ruin crops and damage buildings. People and animals are sometimes washed away by floods.

Types of flood

If there is more rain or melting snow than usual, this extra water runs into rivers and streams. The rivers and streams overflow. Some of the floodwater sinks into the soil. The rest flows back into the river, or dries out in the sun. Seawater can also flood over the land. Very strong winds can cause waves that crash onto the land. High tides at certain times of year can also cause floods along coasts.

Flood defences, like the Thames Barrier in London, England have been built to protect big cities from flooding.

During the floods in the midwest of the United States in 1993, many rivers burst their banks.

People and floods

People have always lived near rivers because they can be used for transport, fishing and washing. The land is good for farming. Many people are at risk from floods. There are different ways to help protect people. Dams are built across rivers to hold back extra water. River banks and sea walls are made higher and stronger. Special diggers called dredgers can make rivers deeper to hold more water.

Flower

See also: Plant, Seed

A flower is the part of a plant that produces seeds. Many flowers have beautiful, coloured petals. Flowering plants grow almost everywhere except for the very coldest places on land.

Life of a flower

The job of a flower is to make new plants. A flower has either male pollen or female ovules, or both. A grain of pollen from one flower joins with an ovule in another flower to produce a seed. The ripe seed may grow into a new plant.

Many people grow flowers because they like them. Some, like sunflowers are grown as a crop. Flowers are specially grown for making perfume.

Sunflowers are grown as a crop, to be sold. Their seeds are used in animal feeds and are crushed for their oil.

FLOWER FACTS

NUMBER OF KINDS OF FLOWERING	
PLANTS	over 250,000
SIZE...........................	up to 90 cm across
LIFESPAN....................	flowering plants can live over 100 years
ENEMIES.....................	fungi, bacteria, some insects, bad weather

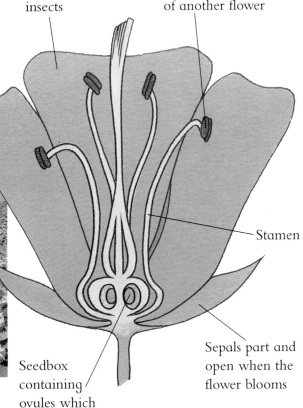

Brightly coloured petals attract insects

Male pollen grains on the anther can join with the female ovules of another flower

Stamen

Seedbox containing ovules which become seeds

Sepals part and open when the flower blooms

The parts of a flower

Fly

See also: Insect, Mosquito

A fly is an insect. Different kinds of fly live all over the world. Many flies carry germs that cause food-poisoning, and diseases such as malaria and sleeping sickness.

Fly families

A fly begins life as an egg. The egg hatches into a maggot which looks like a small worm. When it is fully grown, the maggot changes into a pupa and then into an adult fly. A large group of flies is called a swarm.

FLY FACTS

NUMBER OF	
KINDS..........	about 100,000
COLOUR......	usually black, grey, brown or yellowish
LENGTH......	1.3 mm–7.5 cm
STATUS.......	common
LIFE SPAN....	up to 2 years
ENEMIES......	spiders, birds, people, chemicals called insecticides

A house fly

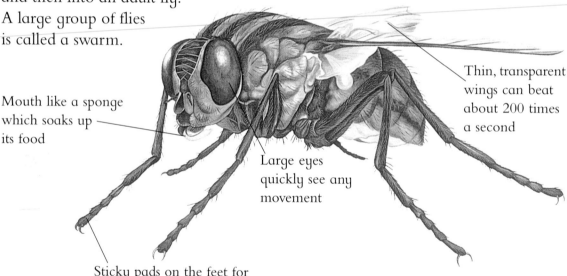

Mouth like a sponge which soaks up its food

Large eyes quickly see any movement

Thin, transparent wings can beat about 200 times a second

Sticky pads on the feet for walking upside-down on the ceiling

FOOD

Some flies, like mosquitoes, bite their prey and suck up a drop of their blood. Other flies, such as house flies, spit on their food and then suck up the spit mixed with the food.

These blowfly maggots are feeding.

Folk music

*See also: Dance, Music,
Musical Instrument*

Folk music started as the
music played or sung by
ordinary people. People
have always liked to sing
together as they worked,
and to listen to other
people.

Folk music today

Today, there are professional folk
musicians who play and sing as a
job. This kind of music is mainly
played on traditional
instruments, like guitars, fiddles,
flutes and harps.

Some people play just for fun, but
there are many well-known folk
groups and musicians who give
concerts.

New folk music

Many traditional folk songs and
tunes have been handed down
through the years from one
musician to another. They are
still popular.

Folk music has also changed
over the years as new
instruments are used and people
find new ways of playing the
tunes. New folk music is always
being written.

*This folk group is performing a concert
out of doors in the United States.*

*Every country in the world has its own
folk music. These musicians are from the
Andean Mountains in South America.*

Cecil Sharp (1859–1924)

The Englishman, Cecil Sharp, was very interested
in traditional folk songs and dances. He visited the
United States in 1916 to collect songs from the
people living in the Appalachian Mountains.
Sharp found the people were singing songs their
ancestors had brought with them from England
300 years before. Some of these songs had
disappeared in England, or no one there knew the
tunes. Now people can look at Sharp's books to
find out more about these songs.

Food chain

See also: Animal, Energy, Plant

All animals need to eat to get energy. Some animals eat other animals. Some animals eat plants. A food chain shows how the energy passes from one creature to another.

From plants to animals

All food chains start with plants. Animals that eat plants are called herbivores. They are the next step in the chain. Animals called carnivores eat other animals and are the next step. Humans are in food chains too. Most humans are omnivores. This means they eat both plants and animals.

Lions are carnivores. They are trying to catch, and eat, the plant-eating wildebeests.

This shows a food chain. The sun helps the rosebush to grow. The aphids eat the bush. The ladybird eats the aphids. The bird eats the ladybird. The cat eats the bird.

Forest

See also: Rainforest, Tree, Wood

A forest is an area where a lot of trees grow close together. Forests cover over one third of all the land on the earth. The amount of forest goes down every year.

Large parts of the Amazon rainforest have been cleared of trees. The land that is left is not always very good for growing crops.

Types of forests

The forests in cold places mainly have coniferous trees, such as firs and pines. These have needle leaves and cones. Deciduous trees grow in warmer areas. They have broad leaves that they drop once a year. Oak, elm, maple and beech trees are deciduous trees. Tropical rainforests grow in places where it is very hot and wet. Forests are homes for many kinds of birds, animals and insects.

People and forests

Forests are important to people because trees make oxygen that people and animals need to breathe. The problem is that people are cutting down forests without planting new trees. They do this to make land for farming or to sell the wood from the trees, for money. In many countries, most of the forests are now gone.

Forests can create just the right conditions for other plants to live on the forest floor. This eucalyptus forest in Australia is also a good place for ferns.

Fossil

See also: Dinosaur, Fuel

Fossils are formed from the remains of dead animals or plants. Looking at fossils tells us about animals and plants that lived a long time ago.

How fossils form

When an animal dies, any bones or shells that are left behind get covered up with mud. Over time, the mud gradually turns to rock. In the rock will be a fossil made of rock or minerals with the same shape as the bone or shell.

What fossils are found?

Some fossils are from creatures that are like animals that are still living today. Many are from animals that died out millions of years ago, like dinosaurs. Fossil bones tell us a lot about the skeletons of dinosaurs.

Plants can leave fossils too. Coal is made from dead plants that have been squeezed hard and heated underground. It is called a fossil fuel.

DID YOU KNOW?

Chalk is a kind of fossil. It is made up of the shells of tiny sea creatures that died millions of years ago.

This fossil is of a fish that lived on earth 200 million years ago.

This scientist is working on a rock face of fossil remains. He will be able to work out when the animals that made the fossils were alive.

Fox

See also: Dog, Mammal

A fox is a meat-eating mammal. It is a member of the dog family. Foxes are found almost everywhere north of the equator.

Fox families

A male fox is called a dog and a female fox is called a vixen. Once a fox has chosen a mate, they stay together for life. The vixen usually has four to five cubs at a time. Foxes dig a home called a den or earth. The dog fox usually hunts for food at night while the vixen looks after the cubs. Female cubs may stay with their parents for a year. Young males leave home when they are about six months old.

FOX FACTS

NUMBER OF KINDS....	21
COLOUR.....	red, grey or white
LENGTH......	up to 80 cm
WEIGHT......	about 10 kg
STATUS........	common
LIFE SPAN....	about 10 years
ENEMIES......	People hunt foxes for sport. Farmers kill foxes to protect chickens.

Long, full tail for warmth when sleeping

Strong legs for running

Sensitive nose to smell food and danger

Sharp claws for digging

An American red fox

FOOD

A fox eats rabbits and small rodents, birds and eggs. Foxes will take chickens from farms. In the autumn, foxes will eat soft fruit.

A female red fox looking after her two cubs in their den in the mountains of Montana in the USA.

France

See also: Europe

France is a country in the west of Europe. There are high mountains in the east and south-west. There are big areas of lowland with wide, winding rivers.

Living and working

Most people live in the towns and cities. France is well known for its food products and its cooking. French cheeses, wine, bread and mineral water are sold all over the world. The main French festival is Bastille Day on 14 July. This is when the people celebrate the 1789 French Revolution.

Most of France is farmland. Farmers grow cereal crops and grapes. Cheese is made from the milk of cows and goats. Cars, aircraft, clothes and other goods are made in factories.

DID YOU KNOW?

The Eiffel Tower was built in 1889. It is named after Alexandre Eiffel who designed it.

The Eiffel Tower is a famous landmark in Paris.

EUROPE

FACT FILE

PEOPLE .... French

POPULATION .... 58 million

MAIN LANGUAGE .... French

CAPITAL CITY .... Paris

MONEY .... Franc

HIGHEST MOUNTAIN ... Mont Blanc – 4807 m

LONGEST RIVER .... River Loire – 1020 km

Frog

See also: Amphibian,
Metamorphosis

A frog is an amphibian. It is born
in the water but spends most of
its life on land. Different kinds of
frog live all over the world. A few
frogs can even climb trees. Most
frogs hide during the day and
come out at night.

Frog families

In spring, a frog lays about 2000-4000
eggs, called frogspawn, in a pond. These
eggs hatch out as tadpoles. Over a few
weeks or months these tadpoles change
into frogs. Most frogs do not look
after their tadpoles. In
cold countries frogs
hibernate in mud
or in leaves during
the winter.

Springy back legs
for jumping

The dark spot in each egg can turn
into a tadpole.

FROG FACTS

NUMBER
OF KINDS.... about 2600
COLOUR..... Poisonous frogs are brightly
coloured. Most other frogs are
brown or green.
LENGTH...... up to 30cm
STATUS....... common
LIFE SPAN ... 5-12 years
ENEMIES ..... foxes, herons, fish and ducks.
Ducks, newts and dragonfly
larvae eat tadpoles.

Eyes that can
look two ways
for danger

Many frogs
have long,
sticky tongues
for catching
insects

Some frogs have webbed
feet for swimming

An American
river frog

FOOD

Tadpoles eat water weed. Bigger
tadpoles eat insects. Adult frogs eat
flies and slugs.

Fuel

See also: Electricity, Energy

A fuel is anything that gives off heat or other forms of energy. Natural gas, oil and coal are all fuels.

Types of fuel

Natural gas comes from gas wells. A deep hole is drilled into the ground and the gas rushes up. Gas can be used for cooking and heating and to make electricity in power stations.

Oil comes from wells in the ground. It is often found in the same places as gas. Crude oil straight from the ground is black and sticky. Oil refineries turn it into useful fuels. Petrol, diesel and heating oil all come from crude oil. Most coal from the ground is burnt in power stations to make electricity.

DID YOU KNOW?

In some places people use a machine that can make fuel out of cow dung.

This peat is being cut and stacked to dry so it can be burnt as a fuel.

People and fuels

One day, all the fuels in the ground will be used up. Scientists are trying to work out ways to use renewable fuels. These are fuels that will not run out. Other sources of fuel energy are the sun and the wind. These will not run out like the fossil fuels from the ground.

At this oil refinery in Kuwait, crude oil is pumped from underground and turned into fuel oil.

Fungus

See also: Plant

A fungus is a living thing like a plant but it has no leaves or stem, and no real roots. Fungi include mushrooms, toadstools, yeasts and moulds. They grow nearly everywhere, on land and in water.

FUNGI FACTS

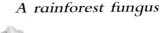

NUMBER OF KINDS	over 100,000
LARGEST FUNGI	up to 30 cm across
LIFE SPAN	some live many years
ENEMIES	bacteria, special chemicals called fungicides

Life of a fungus

The main part of the fungus is under the ground. Tiny threads take in food from the soil. A mushroom is like the fruit of a fungus. A fungus produces spores instead of seeds. The spores are scattered by the wind or by animals. Some fungi grow on living plants and animals.

A rainforest fungus

Gills underneath the mushroom contain the spores

Some fungi cause diseases in people, animals and plants. Other fungi are very useful. Fungi are used to make bread rise, to make yogurt, some cheeses and an important medicine called penicillin. Some mushrooms are eaten as food. Other mushrooms and toadstools are very poisonous.

Tiny fungi grow under trees in forests. Scientists who study fungi like these are called mycologists.

Germany

See also: Europe

Germany is a country in the middle of Europe. The north of Germany is lowland. There are hills and mountains in the centre and south. Big rivers flow through Germany from south to north. It is mostly warm in summer, but it can be very cold with snow in winter.

Living and working

Most people in Germany live and work in the big cities.

There are special traditions and festivals in most towns and villages. Many have to do with local food or customs. Some festivals go back 600 years to medieval times. One of the most famous festivals reminds people of the 'Pied Piper of Hamelin' who cleared that town of rats.

DID YOU KNOW?

From 1948 to 1990 Germany was divided into two countries. The western half was called the German Federal Republic and the eastern half was the German Democratic Republic.

Many towns and cities in Germany have open squares, like this one in the Romer area of Frankfurt.

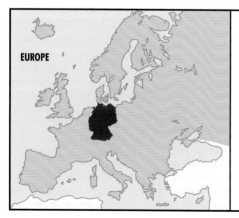

EUROPE

FACT FILE

PEOPLE	Germans
POPULATION	80.3 million
MAIN LANGUAGE	German
CAPITAL CITY	Berlin
MONEY	Deutschmark
HIGHEST MOUNTAIN	Zugspite – 2963 m
LONGEST RIVER	River Rhine – 1320 km

Ghana

See also: Africa

Ghana is a country in west Africa. It is mostly hot lowland. It is cooler in the hills in the east and west of the country. There are two rainy seasons. The world's largest man-made lake is in Ghana.

Living and working

Most people in Ghana live near the coast. Over half the people work on farms in the countryside.

Rice, yams and cassava are grown and eaten with meat, fish and peanut stews. Many Ghanaians wear clothes made of *kente*. This is a special, many-coloured cloth. It is sold in local markets, and also to other countries.

There are also small factories and mines. Cocoa beans grown in Ghana are sent all over the world to be made into chocolate.

Traders bring their produce to local markets to sell. This market is in Kasoa in the central region of Ghana.

DID YOU KNOW?

Ghana used to be part of an area known as the Gold Coast. It took the name 'Ghana' when it became independent in 1957.

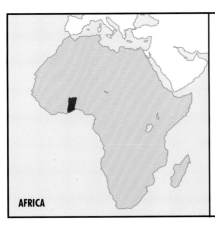

AFRICA

FACT FILE

PEOPLE	Ghanaians
POPULATION	16.9 million
MAIN LANGUAGES	English, African languages
CAPITAL CITY	Accra
MONEY	Cedi
HIGHEST MOUNTAIN	Afadjato – 885 m
LONGEST RIVER	River Volta – 1530 km

Giraffe

See also: Mammal

A giraffe is the tallest land mammal in the world. It lives on the grassy plains of Africa. Every giraffe's coat has a slightly different pattern.

Horns for fighting

A giraffe has to open its legs wide apart to bend low enough to drink.

Long tongue pulls leaves from trees

Giraffe families

A male giraffe is called a bull. A female giraffe is called a cow. A cow has one calf at a time. The females help look after each other's calves. Giraffes do not stay in one special group, but move from group to group. The bulls fight, and the winner becomes the head bull in an area. Because a giraffe moves around, it does not build a home.

GIRAFFE FACTS

NUMBER OF KINDS	1
COLOUR	brown, yellow and white
LENGTH	about 2 m
HEIGHT	up to 5.3 m
WEIGHT	up to 1900 kg
STATUS	some are endangered
LIFE SPAN	about 25 years
ENEMIES	hyenas, leopards, wild dogs

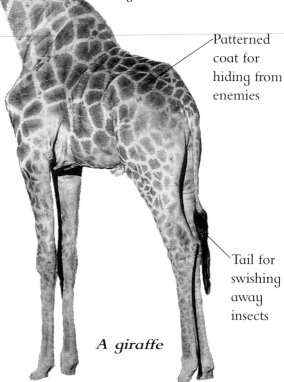

Long neck for reaching leaves high in trees

Patterned coat for hiding from enemies

Tail for swishing away insects

A giraffe

FOOD

A giraffe uses its long neck to reach leaves and shoots from tall trees. It also eats grass.

Goat

See also: Mammal

A goat is a medium-sized mammal. In many parts of the world, people keep goats for their milk, meat and wool. Wild goats live in some mountain areas.

Goat families

A male goat is called a billy goat or a buck. A female goat is called a nanny goat or a doe. A nanny goat usually has two babies at a time. A young goat is called a kid. Farm goats are kept together in groups called herds.

GOAT FACTS

NUMBER OF KINDS	600 (mainly farm goats)
COLOUR	brown, black, white
HEIGHT	45cm–1.2 m
WEIGHT	9–135 kg
STATUS	common
LIFE SPAN	8–10 years
ENEMIES	wolves, bears, lions, leopards

Horns for fighting

An American mountain goat

Shaggy hair is for warmth in cold weather

Strong legs for climbing steep cliffs

FOOD

A goat eats all kinds of plants and fruit, even spiky thorn bushes. Farm goats will eat almost anything, including the labels from tins.

Mountain goats are very sure-footed. From a very young age they can safely trot along narrow ledges.

Goose

See also: Bird

A goose is a large bird, which lives near water everywhere except for the coldest parts of the world. Many kinds of geese migrate long distances each year. Some geese are raised by farmers for their meat, eggs and feathers.

Goose families

A male goose is called a gander and a female is called a goose. A baby goose is called a gosling. A goose and a gander build a nest on the ground and fill it with grass. The goose lays from three to eleven eggs. After the eggs hatch, they both feed the goslings. In the autumn, the family migrates to a warmer area for the winter. They migrate in groups called flocks. The flock flies in a big V-shape, with different geese taking turns to be the leader.

GOOSE FACTS

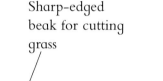

NUMBER OF KINDS	over 30
COLOUR	usually grey, white or black
LENGTH	up to 1.1m
WEIGHT	up to 5kg
STATUS	common
LIFE SPAN	up to 20 years
ENEMIES	foxes, people

Sharp-edged beak for cutting grass

Waterproof feathers for swimming

Strong wings for flying and fighting

Webbed feet for swimming

A Canada goose

FOOD

A goose eats plants in the water and on land.

Snow goose goslings keep warm in a nest lined with their mother's down feathers.

Grasshopper

See also: Insect

A grasshopper is an insect that jumps using its long back legs. It makes a clicking or whirring noise by rubbing its legs or wings. Grasshoppers live in most parts of the world except the Arctic and Antarctica.

GRASSHOPPER FACTS

NUMBER OF KINDS	about 10,000
COLOUR	usually green
LENGTH	up to 11cm
STATUS	common
LIFE SPAN	up to about 9 months
ENEMIES	birds, snakes, frogs, spiders, beetles, people

FOOD

Some grasshoppers eat only one kind of plant. Others eat any plant they can find.

Grasshopper families

A young grasshopper hatches from an egg laid in the soil. The young grasshopper is called a larva. The larva grows and sheds its skin several times, as it slowly changes into an adult with wings. Some grasshoppers form huge groups called swarms.

A short-horned grasshopper

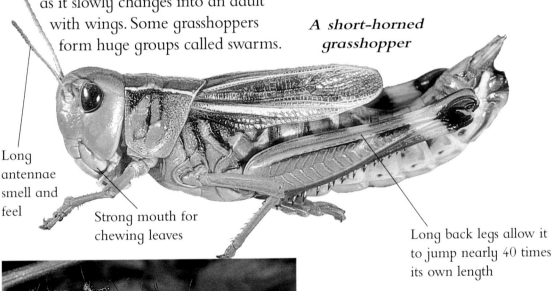

Long antennae smell and feel

Strong mouth for chewing leaves

Long back legs allow it to jump nearly 40 times its own length

These young grasshoppers have a bright warning colour so that their enemies will think they are poisonous and not eat them.

Greece

See also: Europe, Greece (Ancient)

Greece is a country in south-east Europe. Most of Greece is land attached to the rest of Europe. There are also many Greek islands in the Mediterranean Sea.

Living and working

Half of the population of Greece lives in small towns and villages. Many houses are painted white to reflect the hot sun. Olives, grapes, potatoes and sugar beet are grown on small farms.

People from all over the world visit Greece to enjoy the hot, sunny summers and to see the ruins of Ancient Greece. Many Greeks work in the tourist industry in hotels and museums. Some have boats that carry people and goods between the islands.

There are many small fishing boats working around the Greek coast and islands.

DID YOU KNOW?

Greece has a huge shipping fleet. Ships from Greece are used all over the world to transport goods such as grain and oil.

EUROPE

FACT FILE

PEOPLE	Greeks
POPULATION	10.4 million
MAIN LANGUAGE	Greek
CAPITAL CITY	Athens
MONEY	Drachma
HIGHEST MOUNTAIN	Mount Olympus – 2917 m
LONGEST RIVER	River Aliakmon – 290 km

Greece, Ancient

See also: Greece, Olympic Games

Ancient Greece was a civilization that lasted from about 800 BC to 146 BC. For most of the time, Greeks lived in city-states, run in different ways.

What were the Ancient Greeks like?

A city-state included a city and the land around it. Some city-states had one leader. In others the men voted to decide how to run things. All the men had to fight when a city-state went to war. Women ran the homes and brought up the children. The Ancient Greeks believed in many gods and goddesses, and prayed to them and gave them presents to keep them happy.

What are the Ancient Greeks famous for?

The Ancient Greeks are famous for their buildings, statues and painted vases. Their thinkers, writers and inventors are still remembered.

What happened to the Ancient Greeks?

The Romans began to take over Greece in 146 BC. It became part of the Roman Empire.

KEY DATES

800 BC...........The first-city states began

776 BC...........The first Olympic Games were held

700 BC.......... The Greek alphabet was worked out

400 BC.......... The Greeks began to use mathematics

336–323 BC...Alexander the Great ruled all Greece

146 BC...........The Romans took over

The Acropolis, in the city-state of Athens, was a group of buildings on a hill. The largest was this temple called the Parthenon.

Guatemala

See also: Maya, North America

Guatemala is a country in central America. There are lowlands near the coast and to the north of the country. The mountains that cross the middle of Guatemala have very rich soil. There are also active volcanoes in the mountains. Rainforest covers the northern part of the country.

Living and working

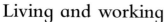

Most people in Guatemala live in small towns and villages in the fertile region, where the soil is good for farming. The farmers grow coffee, sugar, bananas, corn and beans. The chicozapunte tree grows in the northern rainforest. Its sap is used to make chewing gum.

The people in Guatemala eat mixed beans and rice with salads made of avocados, tomatoes and onions. Most bread is made from corn.

Mayans are famous for the brightly coloured cloth and rugs they weave.

DID YOU KNOW?

Over 1000 years ago the northern part of Guatemala was part of the ancient Mayan civilization. Most of the population is still Mayan Indians.

NORTH
AMERICA

FACT FILE

PEOPLE	Guatemalans
POPULATION	10.3 million
MAIN LANGUAGE	Spanish
CAPITAL CITY	Guatemala City
MONEY	Quetzal
HIGHEST MOUNTAIN	Volcán Tajumulco – 4217 m
LONGEST RIVER	Rio Salinas – 480 km

Gull

See also: Bird, Seabird

A gull is a seabird. A gull cannot dive underwater but it can float on water and also fly. Many gulls move away from the sea and live on lakes or rivers. Gulls are found all over the world.

Gull families

Once gulls choose a partner they usually stay together for life. Some build round nests on the beach. Other kinds of gull lay eggs on cliff ledges. A female gull lays two or three eggs once a year. A baby gull is called a chick. Both parents feed the chick. A chick pecks at the adult's beak to let its parent know it needs food.

GULL FACTS

NUMBER
OF KINDS.....85
COLOUR..... white, grey and black
LENGTH...... up to 65 cm
STATUS........common
LIFE SPAN.... up to 30 years
ENEMIES...... rats, people

Curved beak for pulling off bits of food

Waterproof feathers for keeping dry

A herring gull

Webbed feet for walking on sand and paddling through water

This herring gull chick has splotchy markings to help it hide from enemies.

FOOD

A gull eats almost anything it can find. It will even eat meat from dead seals and whales. It breaks the hard shells of mussels and crabs by dropping them to the ground from the sky.

Haiti

See also: Island, North America

Haiti is a country on part of the island of Hispaniola in the Caribbean Sea. It has mountains with small valleys and hot coastal plains. The climate is hot and wet all the year round.

Living and working

Most people in Haiti live in the countryside on very small farms. Coffee, sisal, sugar cane and cocoa are grown to be sold to other countries. Farmers also grow corn, cassava, sweet potatoes and beans for food. There are also mines. Cloth is made in factories.

The life style of the people of Haiti is called Creole. This is a mixture of African and French ways of life. The food, the houses and the music are a blend of things from both cultures. The people also follow both old African religions and Christianity.

During carnival time in Haiti, people dress in costumes and dance through the streets in big processions.

DID YOU KNOW?

About 200 years ago, King Christophe of Haiti started using gourds as money. A gourd is a hard-skinned fruit, like a pumpkin. Even though Haiti now uses coins, the name of the money is still the same.

NORTH AMERICA

FACT FILE

PEOPLE......................... Haitians
POPULATION................ 7 million
MAIN LANGUAGES........ French, Haitian Creole
CAPITAL CITY.............. Port-au-Prince
MONEY........................ Gourde
HIGHEST MOUNTAIN.... Chaîne de la Selle – 2680 m
LONGEST RIVER .... Artibonite River – 160 km

Hare

See also: Mammal, Rabbit

A hare is a mammal that looks like a rabbit, but with long ears and longer legs. It is also called a jackrabbit. Hares live on grassland over much of the world. Some hares live in snowy places. Their fur turns white in the winter.

Hare families

A male hare is called a jack. A female hare is called a doe. The doe has from two to four babies, called leverets, at a time. The doe scrapes a small hollow in the grass. This nest is called a form. She puts grass in the form to make it soft. When she has had her babies she makes each leveret its own form. When the leverets are three weeks old they leave their mother and live on their own.

These European hare leverets are warming themselves in the sun.

HARE FACTS

NUMBER
OF KINDS.... 44 hares and rabbits
COLOUR..... brown, grey or white
LENGTH...... about 60 cm
WEIGHT...... about 5 kg
STATUS........ common
LIFE SPAN.... about 5 years
ENEMIES...... foxes and eagles

Sensitive nose smells danger

Long ears help the hare keep cool and listen out for danger

A black-tailed jackrabbit

Long legs for jumping and for running at up to 70 kph

Strong front paws for fighting

FOOD

A hare feeds at night on grass, roots, bark and cereal crops.

Hawk

See also: Bird

A hawk is a bird of prey. This means that it catches and kills animals to eat. There are many kinds of hawk living all over the world, except in Antarctica.

Hawk families

A female hawk lays her eggs in a nest. After hatching, the chicks stay in the nest and are fed by the parents until they are strong enough to fly. Hawk nests can be on a cliff, in a tree or on the ground.

Curved talons for grasping and carrying prey

Tail for steering while soaring

HAWK FACTS

NUMBER OF KINDS	..... about 200
COLOUR	...... usually brown or grey
LENGTH	...... 25–70 cm
WEIGHT	...... 90 g–2 kg
STATUS	.... some are rare
LIFE SPAN	.... up to 25 years
ENEMIES	...... larger birds, people

Broad wings for soaring through the air

Good eyesight for spotting small animals from high in the air

Sharp, hooked beak for tearing up food

A buzzard

The crested hawk feeds her chicks with insects and frogs.

FOOD

Hawks eat mice, frogs, insects and other small animals. Some hawks swallow all the parts of their prey, including fur, feathers and bones. They then bring up and spit out parts they cannot digest as small lumps called pellets.

Heart

See also: Blood, Human body, Lung

The heart is a pump that pushes blood around the body. It is made of a special sort of strong muscle. Every animal has a heart. In most animals, the heart is in the chest.

Surgeons can perform operations on unhealthy hearts. Special machines take over the work of the heart and lungs while the surgeon operates.

How the heart works

The heart has four spaces in it. The top two are called atria. They fill up with blood that has been around the body through the veins. They then squeeze the blood into the two spaces at the bottom, called the ventricles. Valves, like doors that only open one way, stop the blood going the wrong direction.

The human heart beats more than two billion times in a lifetime. When a person is asleep the heart slows down. If a person exercises, the heart pumps faster.

STAY SAFE!

Eating the proper food, not smoking and taking enough exercise can keep the heart healthy.

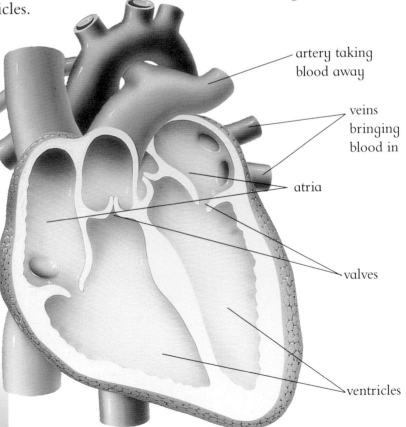

artery taking blood away

veins bringing blood in

atria

valves

ventricles

The human heart

Heat

See also: Energy, Fuel

Heat is a kind of energy. Heat is usually released by burning fuel. There are many types of fuel, for example, firewood or the food we eat.

Types of heat

Heat is important to human beings. If the human body is not warm enough, a person can die.

Materials called insulators keep heat in. When curtains are pulled across windows, the curtains help keep the heat inside the house. People wear warmer clothes in winter to keep their bodies from losing heat. An animal's fur is also a very good insulator. It keeps the animal warm.

Materials called conductors let heat through. Metals are good conductors.

A special camera was used to show the heat escaping from this house. The yellow areas show where most heat is escaping.

People and heat

People have used heat since prehistoric humans first made fires. Heat can be used to soften or melt things, so that their shape can be changed. Metals and some plastics can be shaped using heat in this way.

Saucepans are made of metal so heat passes from the cooker to the food. The handle is an insulator. This stops the hand being burned.

Hedgehog

See also: Mammal

A hedgehog is a mammal. A hedgehog's body is covered in spines. When it is in danger it can roll into a ball and protect itself. Hedgehogs are found in woods and fields in parts of Europe, Asia, Africa and New Zealand.

HEDGEHOG FACTS

NUMBER OF KINDS	12
COLOUR	brown
LENGTH	20–30 cm
WEIGHT	about 700 g
STATUS	common
LIFE SPAN	about 6 years
ENEMIES	foxes, road traffic

Hedgehog families

A male hedgehog lives on his own. A female hedgehog builds a special nest in spring or summer for her four to six babies. After four weeks the babies leave the nest. Some hedgehogs in cold places build nests of leaves where they hibernate all winter.

Good ears for hearing worms and insects.

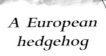

A European hedgehog

Long nose for smelling out food on the ground

Sharp spines for protection

Little feet can be tucked inside when it rolls into a ball

Hedgehog babies are born with soft spines that quickly harden.

FOOD

A hedgehog hunts for worms and insects at night. It also likes soft fruit.

Helicopter

See also: Aeroplane, Transport

A helicopter is an aircraft without fixed wings. Spinning blades, called rotors, on top of the helicopter, push it up into the air. Helicopters were first thought of hundreds of years ago, but were not built until this century.

The first helicopters

The first helicopter was built in 1907. It went out of control very easily. By 1937, helicopters had improved and could fly properly. They were first used by the army in the United States. Most helicopters are still used by military forces.

How we use helicopters

Helicopters can land almost anywhere. They can take off straight up into the air, go forwards, backwards and sideways. They can also hover over the same spot. Because of these features they are very useful where there is not room to land an aeroplane. They can be used to rescue people from sinking ships or mountain cliffs. Helicopters can be used as ambulances and they can be used by the police to chase criminals where cars can't go.

HELICOPTER FIRSTS

FIRST INVENTED	1907
FIRST MILITARY HELICOPTERS	1942
FIRST PASSENGER HELICOPTERS	1945
FIRST TRANSATLANTC HELICOPTER FLIGHT	1967

In 1907, Frenchman Paul Cornu's double rotor machine crashed almost every time it tried to take off.

An ambulance helicopter can travel very quickly and land in places ambulances cannot reach.

Hibernation

See also: Animal, Season

Some animals have a type of winter sleep called hibernation. In the cold of winter there is not much food around. When the weather gets warmer, the animal wakes up again.

How does hibernation work?

Hibernation is not just going to sleep. The heart slows right down in some hibernating animals. The animal's breathing is very light and slow. It almost seems dead. When it is time, it can take days for the animal to wake up completely. Hibernating animals need to hide away in a safe place, so that their enemies can't find them. Before they go to sleep, they eat a lot. The fat on their bodies keeps them alive while they sleep.

This black bear in its den has been woken from its hibernation.

Who hibernates?

Many different kinds of animals hibernate. Butterflies and other insects will sometimes creep into sheds and garages. Bats hibernate in the caves and roofs where they roost. Snakes and other reptiles also hibernate. Frogs and toads bury themselves in mud or piles of leaves.

Some animals hide away in the winter, but don't really hibernate. Squirrels stay in their nests and rest for most of the winter, but they come out on fine, warm days.

This hedgehog has been hibernating under a pile of leaves.

Hieroglyphics

See also: Alphabet, Aztecs, Egypt (Ancient), Maya

Hieroglyphics are a kind of writing that uses pictures. The most ancient styles of writing that have been discovered all used some form of hieroglyphics.

Who used hieroglyphics?

The Ancient Egyptians, the Mayans and the Aztecs all used hieroglyphics. They carved them on to stone or painted them onto stone or paper.

Hieroglyphics were useful to show real things, but were hard to use for showing ideas. The pictures had to be drawn almost exactly the same way each time, or people reading them would have been confused. Drawing or carving hieroglyphics took a long time, and they were hard to learn. Only a few people could read or write using them.

What happened to hieroglyphics?

Over time, groups who used hieroglyphics gradually changed them to show whole words, then sounds that were used to build up words. Alphabets took over from hieroglyphics because they were clearer and were quick and easy to learn.

KEY DATES

4000 BC.... The first alphabet was worked out.

3000 BC.... The Egyptians began to use hieroglyphics

AD 500...... The Maya began to use hieroglyphics

AD 1200.... The Aztecs began to use hieroglyphics

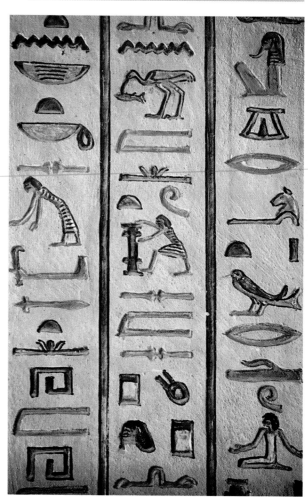

Egyptian hieroglyphics were used to tell people something about the person buried inside a tomb.

Hinduism

See also: India

Hinduism is the oldest world religion. It began in India about 4000 years ago. Its followers are called Hindus.

Beliefs and teachings

Hindus believe that in life everyone has duties, called dharma. These include things like worshipping God and not hurting other people. Hindus think it is important to lead a good life.

Hindus believe in a great power called Brahman. They worship Brahman through many gods. In Hinduism each god has special powers over such things as money or childbirth. Some important gods are Krishna, Shiva and Vishnu. The Hindu beliefs and teachings are written down in holy books called the Vedas.

This statue of Krishna is decorated with flowers.

Hinduism today

There are now over 805 million Hindus. Nearly half live in India. Hindus worship and pray in their homes and at temples. There are many important Hindu festivals. One festival is Divali, the festival of light. This is when Hindus celebrate stories of the gods overcoming evil.

Festivals, like this one in honour of the god Shiva, are important in Hinduism.

Hippopotamus

See also: Mammal

A hippopotamus is a very heavy land mammal. Only the elephant is heavier. Hippopotamuses only live in central Africa. Most of the daytime, hippopotamuses soak in water. When it is cooler at night, they come out to eat grass.

Hippopotamus families

Female hippos and their children live in a group of 15–20. Each group has one adult male. Other adult males live together in a group. A baby can swim and walk as soon as it is born. A young hippo lives with its mother and older brothers and sisters for several years.

Eyes, ears and nose on the top, so it can go almost under the water and still see, hear and breathe

Big teeth for fighting, little teeth for munching grass

HIPPOPOTAMUS FACTS

NUMBER OF KINDS	2
COLOUR	brown
LENGTH	up to 3.3 m
HEIGHT	1.5 m
WEIGHT	up to 3,200 kg
STATUS	common
LIFE SPAN	up to 50 years
ENEMIES	Crocodiles sometimes kill baby hippos.

A hippopotamus

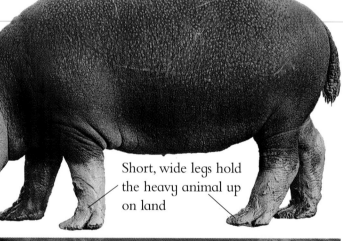

Short, wide legs hold the heavy animal up on land

FOOD

A hippopotamus can walk up to three kilometres every night looking for fresh grass.

During the day while the hippos soak in water, the babies are kept safe on top of the adults.